VISIT THE AUTHOR AT

A Soul-Full World

NOURISHING YOUR SPIRITUAL LIFE

ASOULFULLWORLD.COM

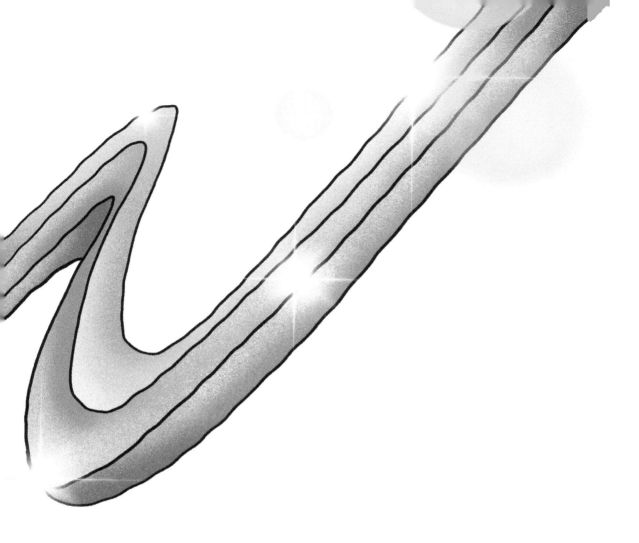

Interior Image Credit: April Lavely-Robinson
Graphic Design: Rhett Kirgis and Mike Reid

ISBN: 978-1-954047-69-3 (sc)
ISBN: 978-1-954047-70-9 (hc)
ISBN: 978-1-954047-68-6 (e)

Library of Congress Control Number: 2021906397

Dear Reader,

Preparing for change is an important step, no matter what age you are. This whimsical story embraces change as a joy-filled and beautiful adventure. It's a story about a strong and steadfast mountain and her journey to discover her inner light. Along the way, she must release old ideas about who she is and recognize who she is becoming. No matter what age you are, this book is for you – and those you love.

Nature has been talking to me all my life. As a child, I often laid in the grass, with my hands propping up my chin, so I could watch the sprites that lived under the heads of flowers in my mother's garden beds. They were as real to me as the birds and bugs I spent hours watching move between blades of grass. Perhaps you had similar experiences.

The Changing Story was told to me by the Arkansas River, at a location where it flows through Colorado. She (the river) asked me to put into words what came to me in visions. A few years later, April Lavely-Robinson, the book's talented illustrator, miraculously showed up in my life to complete the project. She gave the book its unique elegance and beauty - and added details I saw but never shared with her. It was a mystical experience for both of us.

This book will help people of all ages - and especially children - to understand that, over time, we "change, and change, and change again, to become who we truly are." Imagine how your life might have been different if you had received this message as a child.

I'm a parent of five boys and a grandma several times over, so I know how challenging it can be to read the same "favorite" story again and again, keeping it interesting for reader and listener alike. I've included a glossary of all the symbols woven into The Changing Story in the back of the book. Readers can explore the glossary and engage children in new characters and the meaning of various symbols every time they read it. This keeps the experience and the interaction new, lively, and fun. I've also included a few drawing pages that invite children to share more with you about change and what they see in nature.

My greatest hope is that reading The Changing Story will not only help children to experience change in a positive way but will also help you to remember your own childhood connection to nature and allow you to see the beauty of change in your life.

Soul-full blessings,

Rev. Dr. Ahriana Platten – Author

asoulfullworld.com

This book is dedicated to my beloved husband, Mark, who shares my love of nature and hears Her voice - and to my children and grandchildren who are continually teaching me to play.

The Changing Story

Written by Ahriana Platten

Illustrated by April Lavely-Robinson

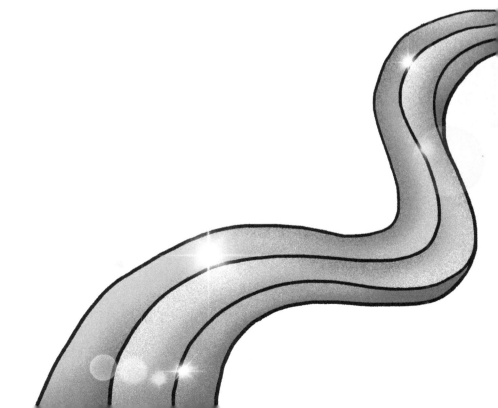

It's rare for me to recline on a warm stone at the side of a river, but, on this particular day, that's exactly what I did.

The sun was soothing, and the river was fresh with run-off from a recently fallen snow. It was a very special day. I was about to hear a *Story* and the teacher who told it splashed and gurgled beside me as I closed my eyes to listen.

There once was a great mountain.
Oh yes, all mountains are great,
but this mountain was

Magnificent!

Tall and proud, she stood firm
in her station. She was a mighty
being with a grand air
of permanence.

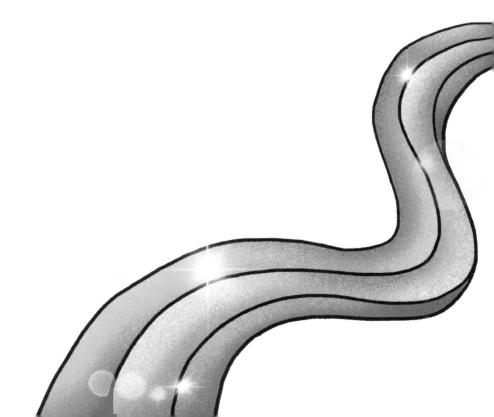

The deer who visited told her about
grassy valleys where they grazed,
and she pondered the places she
had never seen.

The butterflies spoke about sunbeams
that danced on the surface of the river
and the Mountain imagined their beauty.

The birds spoke of a Wondrous place
where the water stretched on and on
forever, and the shore glistened like stars
in the ebony night.

The Mountain wished she could see
it herself, but hers was the job of
stillness and strength.

One day, as she stood her ground, she felt a tap… tap… tap against her skin.

The gentle rain whispered to her "It's Time to Change."

"I am a Mountain, strong and stable. I stay the same," she said.

"It's time to change, as all things must" said the rain.

Tiny droplets fell, becoming ticklish trickles, then rivulets formed, loosening chunks of rock that rolled downhill, coaxed by the rain's relentless current.

"Oh my! I am a Boulder," said the Mountain, as she tumbled to the valley... and the deer, recognizing the Mountain in its new form, said "welcome, friend!", while the lanky green grass made a swoosh, swoosh sound as the Boulder rolled by.

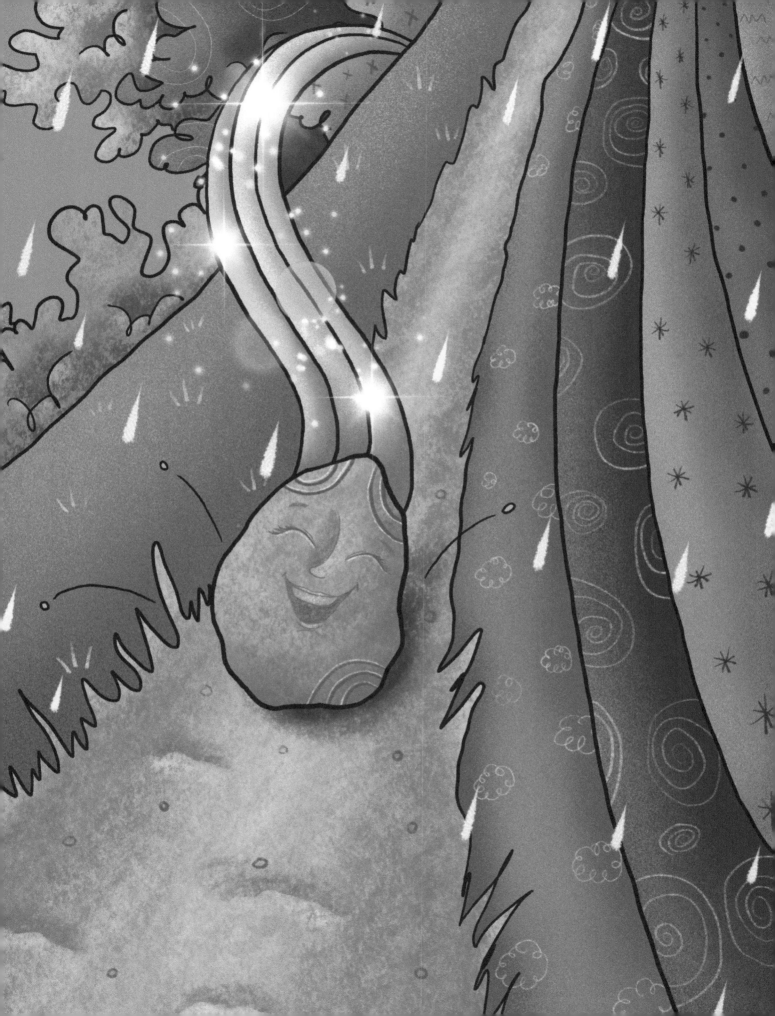

The Boulder rolled into the river with a *Sploosh*, sending a smaller piece of itself into the watery current.

From under the water, it looked up to see the sunbeams glistening above it. "I am a Stone," said the Mountain joyfully, and the butterflies, recognizing the Mountain in its new form, said "welcome, friend," as they danced a *Lively Jig.*

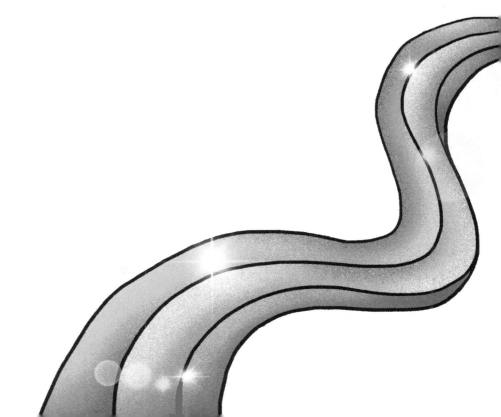

Onward the Stone tumbled, taking on a dance of its own, splintering into smaller and smaller Pebbles.

It rushed downstream, until finally, the river carried it right into the mighty sea.

"I am the tiniest grain of Sand," said the Mountain as it washed up on the shore. And the birds, recognizing the Mountain in its new form, said "welcome, friend! Look how you sparkle and shine like a star in the night sky!"

Hearing these words, the Mountain noticed its unique *Beauty* for the first time!

"I am your *Mother Ocean*" a tender voice said. "You are home, child. You were born a mighty Mountain and you might have remained only that had you been unwilling to change. Being a Mountain is a noble thing indeed, yet those who stand still see so little of life."

"Your courage moved you forward."

"Bit by bit, you surrendered your certainty and tumbled willy-nilly to explore the greatest mystery of all

- The Vast Unknown.

You journeyed on the river of life, releasing all that you thought you were, in order to become the brilliant essence that exists at your very core."

"And now, you have arrived here...
a diamond whirling in the ebb and flow,
comforted and *Loved* by each wave that
greets you."

"I am the Light," said the Mountain.

"Yes," said the Ocean, "the Light has always been inside of you. The Winds of Change came to reveal your inner truth."

"Welcome my child", she said, then she sang a lullaby that can only be heard by those who are willing to Change, and Change, and Change again to become who they really are.

The End

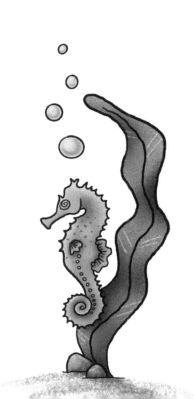

This Story was a gift from Nature. The illustrations are chock full of symbols that can deepen its meaning. Whether you are reading it for yourself, reading it to your little ones, or gifting it to someone who is changing, we hope you find it inspiring and uplifting. Please enjoy this glossary of suggested meanings for the symbols within this story.

Animal Symbols

Bird: Serenity, peace and diligence

Butterflies: Transformation, beauty

Deer: Gentleness, grace, ability to be agile and change direction

Earthworms: Underground emotions

Fish: Spiritual change

Fox: Seeing through deception, the ability to be discerning. Rest along the way.

Jellyfish: Dreams, healing painful memories

Owl: Intelligence, seeing through the truth hidden in the darkness

Rabbit: Creativity, observation and fertility

Spider: Weaving the web of life, experiential understanding

Whale: Wise teachers who show up along the path of change

Nature Symbols

Clouds: Mobility, coming and going, shape-shifting

Flowers: Blossoming in beautiful ways as we change

Moon: The Intuition that guides us. You might also call it inner knowing.

Mountain, Boulder, Stone, Sand, Light: The Changing Human who releases ideas about the self in order to bring forth authenticity

Ocean: The ebb and flow of life. What is old meeting what is new.

Rain: Our joys and our sorrows – the motivation for change

River: The power that breaks down our limitations - such as the way a river carved the Grand Canyon

Sea plants: Being in the flow

Stars: Universal acceptance - the stars shine on all of life

Sun: Energy, clarity, being called forth to growth

Trees and Bushes: Witnesses who observe and support all life, and our journey

Vines: The growth that will eventually cause the wall to crumble

Other Symbols

Key: The ability to unlock something new

Labyrinth: A place of change and inspiration

Sparkles: The Great Mystery

Skeleton: The cycle of endings that leads to beginnings

Spiral: The journey of life

Tri-colored ribbon: The Winds of Change moving us onward

Wall: Something that stands between us and change

Window: The opening though which we see change coming

Yemaya: The Ocean Mother who lives along the shores where the water touches the sand, symbolic of the nurturing energy of love and connection. She is especially fond of the innocent and authentic in each of us.

Ahriana Platten – Author

Nature has been talking to Ahriana all her life. When she was little, she laid down in the grass, with her hands propping up her chin, so she could see the sprites that lived under the heads of flowers in her mother's garden beds. She spent hours, nose so close to the ground that she could smell the sweet soil, watching the creatures that moved and lived between blades of grass. Even as an adult, nature brought her comfort. At 39, after a dramatic and painful life change, she took her heartache and climbed into the boughs of a tall cottonwood tree who became her greatest healer, friend and teacher. This story was told to Ahriana in 2007 by the Arkansas River, at the place where it flows through Salida, Colorado. A mystical collaboration with April Lavely-Robinson, the book's talented illustrator, created a moving vision of what Ahriana heard, and gave unique elegance and beauty to the story. It is Ahriana's great desire that this book will help all of us understand that we must "be willing to change, and change, and change again, to become who we truly are." For more information about Ahriana, visit ASoulFullWorld.com.

April Lavely-Robinson - Illustrator

Illustrator April Lavely-Robinson has had a deep love of art her entire life. She fondly remembers sitting at her school desk with a fresh, white sheet of paper neatly laid before her, recalling the excitement that brewed in her soul and an eagerness to create. Through life changes of her own, art has been her constant; her calm place. When Ahriana Platten approached April with the opportunity to illustrate her book, The Changing Story, she was not only honored but felt pulled to complete the task. With each illustration April contemplated Ahriana's words and how they fit into her own life. She has come to realize change is not something to fear but to welcome. April is a proud native of Colorado Springs where she resides with her husband and two children. Visit April's online gallery at www.foxandthetoad.com

What would you like to change in your life? Draw or write about it.

Beyond your own life, if you could change something about the world, what would it be? Draw or write about it.

Does anything in nature speak to you? Draw or write about it.

Printed in the USA
CPSIA information can be obtained
at www.ICGtesting.com
LVHW061342260524
781189LV00003B/100